Inner Prayer

Inner Prayer

Pray within you
and
set every word aglow,
by being totally tranquil
and aligned with the
Inner Light,
with God

Gabriele Wittek

Published by:
© Universal Life
The Inner Religion

P. O. Box 2221 – Deering, NH 03244

U S A

Licensed edition
translated from the original German title:
"Inneres Beten"
Order No. S 307en

From the Universal Life Series
with the consent of
© Verlag DAS WORT GmbH
im Universellen Leben
Max-Braun-Str. 2
97828 Marktheidenfeld/Altfeld, Germany

The German edition is the work of reference
for all questions regarding the meaning
of the contents

ISBN 1-890841-11-0

Those who truly pray find their way to the basis of the heart, to God. In the very source of all Being, they unite with all people and beings. United with God and all Being, they go out into the world to announce the message of love to all seekers of truth, so that all people and beings can find their way to the truth, to the basis of the heart, God.

May all people and beings consciously draw closer to this unity, the universal life.

Gabriele

Contents

How do I reach true prayer?

More and more people, especially the younger generation, are searching and asking for the meaning of life. They are looking for a meaningful existence and can find it only with difficulty. Many are bored with a life of material well-being; it is no longer able to satisfy them. They suffer from material abundance, from the push and pressure of wanting to be and to have. In view of the many threatening and alarming developments that are coming to a head, they increasingly sense that all conditions essential for life are in danger.

And so, many of our fellow brothers and sisters are searching for the truth. Their inner unease, their searching and striving, is deep-rooted. The soul, which is not of this world, senses its eternal home where there is secureness and safety. The soul senses its connection with heavenly beings, among whom happiness, contentment, harmony and love prevail. Without the person being aware of it, the searching soul also longs for the dual unity, for its dual partner, who may live far from this earth in the light-filled spheres of the eternal home.

Soul and person are continuously on a journey. Untiringly, the wanderer strives for new goals that promise fulfillment. Once these goals have been reached, however, there is but a brief rest, fulfillment and satisfaction are of short duration. Nowhere can soul and person find the deep secureness, nowhere the lasting home.

The awakened soul feels that it is merely on a journey. It feels and senses higher things. This pressing sensation and longing of the soul awaken the person. The person who is awakening to spirituality begins to search for the higher, the nobler, and more perfect. The striving of the soul, which wants to reach its origin, makes itself known to the person; it penetrates him and rises in him like the invigorating sap in a tree when springtime draws near.

The awakened soul already hears the calling Spirit. Caringly and lovingly, the Spirit encourages the soul like a mother bird who tries to stir her fledgling to leave its nest in order to learn to fly. "Come," she encourages. "Come and use your wings. Join in the element, which is your life! Experience the freedom and vastness which is your home!" In the same way, the Spirit calls and encourages the awakened soul to climb higher, to walk into the eternal life, which is its own.

The person does indeed sense the longing urge of the soul. The call of the Spirit, "Come follow Me," vibrates into his consciousness more and more. However, the light of the inner being is not yet able to completely penetrate through the veil of the haze of this human world; the primordial melody of life is not yet able to prevail over the loud noise of the world; the intellect still overlies the spiritual sensations, the gentle voice of the eternal truth.

The person turns now here, now there, in order to find what his heart is seeking so restlessly, and has to recognize that he cannot find it externally. But where is there a place for the spiritual life in the crowding, rushing restlessness of our fast-moving time?

Possessions, recognition and pleasure are the standards of an affluent society. They characterize the thinking and acting of today's people. Since such an orientation is contrary to a spiritual life, many people believe that a spiritual life is closed to the one who lives in this world.

Through our professional and social intertwinements, we are all connected with the life of this world. This external life stresses and burdens us more than ever. A person is not able to free himself from it. Technology offers him manifold and ever new opportunities: sensual stimulations and sounds, fascinations and distractions of all kinds, which often exceed the capacity of the individual. The quiet and inwardness that the soul calls for seems to many people like a utopia that has no room for realization in our restless world.

However, this seems so only to the one who thinks that one has to withdraw from the noisy hustle and bustle, from society and profession, in order to attain restfulness. The hustle and bustle of this world may very well have fascinated and captivated many people. The worldly person may very well be bound by what attracts his efforts and striving; this is so today, as it was at all times.

However, the renewal of a person from within, by recalling the powers latent in him, is possible today just as it has been at all times.

We do not have to withdraw from our daily life, from our profession and from society in order to find tranquillity within ourselves. We only have to realize what is important:

To live *in* this world, but not to be *with* this world.

It all depends on what forces we allow to govern us. It all depends on what forces we allow to dominate us and our life. When we are oriented toward the world, toward the material, then the world, all external aspects, will influence us. We will then be children of the world and will take part in everything that is a part of the outer world. Even though the spiritual reality is present as well, it cannot effectively support us, inspire and guide us, because we have not turned toward it; we have not made a conscious connection with it; we have not offered our hand to it.

When we turn toward the spiritual, the external world with its manifestations loses its influence. Although it is still there, it no longer has power over us, since we have offered our hand to the divine in us. The divine now consciously nourishes us, guides and governs us. We may now rest in Him.

Once we have established ourselves in the spiritual life which is within us, the eternal Being will be the firm ground on which we stand. Firmly rooted in this ground and trusting in the powers which stream to us from there, we can grow from it into the external life, in word and deed. The storm of time can indeed shake us but cannot in the end do any harm to us, since we receive strength and power of resistance from the very basis of the eternal Being. And so, we may rest in the Spirit, while fulfilling our task in the world.

As a result of the progressive spiritual ignorance of people, many think that the material and the spiritual, the religious, are two spheres very far from each other. In reality, the coarse, the material spheres of existence here on earth are closely linked with the fine-material, spiritual spheres. They are planes of vibration existing side by side and simultaneously. They penetrate each other: Despite their different frequencies, the existence of one reality does not exclude that of the other— similarly as light and sound can exist together in the same space.

For this reason, we can live very well in this world without, however, being with this world. We just have to decide to give priority to the inner reality of all Being, to the divine. A person who is not with this world but only lives in this world will place what is higher and more noble above what is base, above materialism, thus finding his way to inner tranquillity. But someone who lives in this world and orients himself toward it, that is, who is with this world, will not have his heart filled with inner peace, because this world does not know the peace that streams from the deep source of divine power.

The connection between the material and the spiritual levels of Being is established through devotion. When we turn to the powers of eternal life, an uninterrupted stream of power flows, for God, our Father, never closes His source of primordial power to us.

Prayer is devotion. The person who prays closes the circle of life. The one who prays rightly each day, from his heart, will maintain his inner peace even in the greatest uproar.

There is much spiritual knowledge in this world, but little actualization and even less fulfillment of the heart and the soul!

The knowing person recognizes that in our time the primordial powers of life radiate increasingly into the souls of people in order to awaken them to spirituality. Thus, many people come to recognize the powerlessness and instability of external values, of external existence. Many people are no longer satisfied with possessing something and being someone. The bread of the external, of the material, no longer satisfies many, and they recognize that the external values merely distract and scatter, offering no substance for their life.

All too often they prove to be hollow, stale and ephemeral. They impoverish the heart and bring no stillness or peace.

Where can the soul and the person find the bread of life? Wherever we search, with friends, in this or that place, at external festivities or meetings, we do not find it, if not within us, in our inner being. Many are driven, for the awakened soul urges them; however, they still search where they cannot find, and they deafen themselves in this world. They are incapable of perceiving what is so near to them! And when they hear of it, this often does not help them, because their intellect, their mind which is oriented toward material reality, still rejects and discards.

However, the forces from highly vibrating cosmic spheres strive unceasingly to awaken and vivify. Their activity on our planet can be recognized everywhere and in many forms, for the Spirit of God acts in manifold ways in order to bring home to many people an awareness of their spiritual origin that opens the way to the universal life. Each one of us is guided in such a way that several times in his life on earth he is given the opportunity to recognize what is needed: to recognize that he is a part of the eternal spiritual Being and that it is his task to seek and develop again this origin within himself.

The day when the person realizes who he truly is and finds himself is of decisive significance for his life, that life which does not end with the termination of this journey on earth. It is the day on which he consciously turns to the eternal spiritual life. The person realizes that tranquillity, contentment and the forces of infinite fullness, which are given to him to open up through the divine all-love, are effective only in him, in his inner being.

Our Father, the eternal Spirit, has placed in each soul everything that He, the life, has brought forth and continuously brings forth as power and fullness. This fullness of spiritual power more or less slumbers in us. It wants to be awakened by us. However, if we want to attain inner peace and deep stillness, we have to first become aware of our spiritual origin, for every person is a child of the All-Highest, and shall become again a pure being, a conscious son or daughter of the infinitely eternal life.

The right prayer leads us home to our origin, into the kingdom of eternal light, where happiness, peace, harmony and bliss are waiting for us. Prayer is the bridge to the reality of the Spirit, to the life, which makes us free.

Thus, there is immeasurable power in prayer, since it connects us with the source of the power of life, with the omnipotence of infinity, with God, our Father.

God is love. In prayer we are increasingly grasped by the eternal flow of power of divine love, which is able to bear us upward to the loving consciousness of spiritual life, all the way to the heart of our infinitely eternal Father.

However, the right way to pray has to be learned.

It is not lip-prayers that lead us to the promised land of inner life. Words spoken without sensations do not open the floodgates of the inner being, which then bring the stream of eternal love to flow. It is not the wording, the length of the prayer or any other external characteristic, which is decisive. It is not in the word, in the letter, or in the sound alone that the power lies.

The right prayer takes shape from within. It streams from the soul and the heart. In right prayer the child addresses its Father in its inner being, that is, the child speaks to its inner God, until the floodgates open up through which the soul and heart then pray.

But how do I come to right prayer, to the divine consciousness, which constantly knocks at the heart of a person and wants to reveal to him the inner fullness, the true origin? How do I come to the eternal reality, to the life that makes me free?

The one who seeks will find. However, we cannot find the divine reality, the true peace and the stillness so longed for, outside of our consciousness, in this world.

In order to find this longed-for peace, this secureness and steadfastness, we must first find the way to ourselves. We should believe, that is, accept as truth and confirm in ourselves, that we are not beings of this world, but beings on a journey heavenward, to the Kingdom of Peace.

Jesus of Nazareth said: "The Kingdom of God is within, in you." And so, we have to go into our inner being in order to find the peace and the love, for only the kingdom of the inner being, our eternal homeland, our original home, can give us this peace and this stillness again. To find the way to ourselves means: Recognize yourself!

Simple and plain as this sentence may seem, it becomes demanding for the one who sets out to actualize it. For nearly every one of us sees his surroundings and his fellow man through the window of his own ego. He looks, examines, evaluates and judges according to his very own criteria. There are many things and even many a person displeasing to us, and we think and speak about them accordingly.

To find the way to ourselves means to no longer think negatively about our neighbor. Neither should we talk about him, how he is dressed, about his short-comings, about the extent of his possessions, about what he does or says. We should look at ourselves and recognize our own faults and weaknesses, for what we find fault with in our neighbor is still in ourselves.

This fact, that there is in ourselves a correspondence to what we dislike in the other person, is a fundamental truth on the path of self-recognition. It is not easy for us to accept this fact at first.

Nevertheless, it is so, and soon it will be confirmed everywhere we go: What we emit from our inner being is what we then discover outside of ourselves. Thus, each one has his world, totally in his own way. And from what streams back to him, he can easily and surely recognize what he had sent out before.

If we would emit only love and were thus imbued with divine love, then only love would be expressed toward us. However, when we preoccupy ourselves with our neighbor, with what we dislike about him, with how he thinks and acts or with the way he is dressed, we can draw the conclusion that similar things are in us. For if we were imbued with the love of God, we would emit only selflessness and love. But if envy, hatred and egocentricity are in us, we will always emit what is still in us.

We mostly project these onto our fellow man, thinking that it is our neighbor, our colleague, our fellow man, who is tainted by this or that evil.

But in reality, we are what we want to attribute to our neighbor. For this reason, we should look at ourselves and recognize our own faults and weaknesses, in order to penetrate closer to our eternal being, which is our true life.

Let me repeat. The law of correspondence says: As long as we dislike something about our neighbor, it still marks our nature, too; it is still present in ourselves.

Only through a disciplined life, by attuning ourselves consistently with the divine commandments and thereby with God, the spirit of our inner being, will our soul as well as each cell of our body attain peace and harmony, the consolidation in the awareness of God.

When we are able to find our way inward to the Kingdom of Peace more and more, to our original home, by way of the right prayer and meditation, we will be fully irradiated and guided by the eternal power in us and will be nourished and given drink by the life source of divine peace.

If we then place our trust more and more in the origin of our being, in God, we will become free from our human limitation, brought about by our intellectual thinking, by our feeling and wanting. We then become peaceful, harmonious and happy from within.

In order to find the origin of the wellspring, it is necessary to fight with ourselves. We must discard whatever hinders us from finding our way to where there is peace and harmony, where happiness and security stream through our whole being.

If we want to find peace, we should not plunge into the restlessness and bustle of this world. As often as possible, we should withdraw from all sounds and noises of this world.

If it is possible for us to arrange a quiet room where we just pray and meditate, where we can have a dialogue with the divine, then this room will become a temple of divine harmony. A walk in a quiet forest of evergreen trees can also give us the blissful stillness to penetrate deeper into the realm of eternal peace. Nature gives so much strength and love to the conscious pilgrim; for nature serves the person who longs for God, for His stillness and His peace, giving him powers upon powers. When we perceive nature with our external senses alone, then it reveals to us only its outer appearance. The grass, the flowers and the larger plants appear to be silent. Only the singing of the birds is

31

an indication to us that there is life in the trees.

But in reality every blade of grass, every leaf, every needle of a fir tree sings the song of inner power. When we sit down on a bench or on a rock, away from the worldly bustle, and let the stillness of the forest, the stillness of our surroundings, have an effect on us, then we communicate with the harmonious and harmonizing forces of nature.

A person who practices this exercise frequently will come to realize that true prayer is eternal silence. When all neg-ative thoughts have come to rest and our inner being rises toward the source of life, then right prayer takes place. Then praying is no longer thinking, but sensing the all-power in us, around us, and in all Being.

To find the rest in God means to meet Him silently in us and in all Being.

God is the stillness.

It is said about Jesus that He withdrew into the stillness of nature to communicate with His Father. He recommended the same to His friends and to all of us. He advised them and us to seek out a small quiet chamber, in order to hold a dialogue there with the Almighty. A true dialogue with God is deep, conscious, silent, selfless prayer.

So let us follow His instructions and withdraw for prayer into an undisturbed room or corner where the noise of the world, the harsh, coarse vibration of a noisy earthly life, is silent.

But we should not be deceived by monastic practices, as a result of which many people think we must flee into a monastery or convent or a cell, in order to find inner stillness. This would be just to flee from ourselves. It is not the flight from ourselves that leads us to God, but the return to ourselves, to the cell of our heart.

How do we find our way into this outer and inner stillness? We should first learn right silence, in order to attain a calm, harmonious body rhythm. Silence does not mean to merely close our mouth and not express our thoughts, while retaining and moving them in us. Such a silence would be an external silence and would not bring us into the stillness.

The right silence means to let go of our thoughts about external things and people, about possessing, about money transactions, about meetings with our boss and with unpleasant colleagues. The right silence means to empty ourselves of everything trifling, of everything that preoccupies us again and again, which ultimately is our base self, our base nature.

When we learn to examine and control our thinking and speaking and to distinguish the unessential from the essential, we will also succeed in coming into the right stillness, into the emptiness of thought that we need, so that the Spirit can fill us with His powers, with His love and wisdom.

How do we attain the right prayer, the perpetual inclusion of God in all things, the stillness into which God, the stillness itself, speaks?

Again and again, we collect our thoughts and surrender them to God in order to become still. In this process of collecting our thoughts and surrendering the human in us, we practice the right concentration.

In order to find our way to the true, deep prayer, there is no need for the usual practices and ceremonies of prayer. We need not fold our hands or put them together or even kneel down. For praying, we need not go to external places especially provided for this, like, for instance, churches. We also need not learn prayers by heart, nor say them after someone or read them. We have to become the prayer; it should pray within us. Words merely rambled on do not reach God. What constitutes the prayer is not the words of our human language nor the beautifully formed, well-considered sentences; but the right prayer is the sensations, the vibrations of our soul and of our heart.

Plain or even awkward words often express more than an intellectual prayer of elaborated sentences. God hears only the longing of our heart, the deep resonance of our soul.

We need not keep to specific times for prayer, for God is omnipresent always and everywhere. He is constantly ready to accept the language of the soul and of the heart from His children. He, the Almighty, perceives the impulses of our heart and blesses and fortifies us according to our devotion to Him.

The right prayer is the continuous nearness to God in sensations and thoughts. It is the prayer of the depths, which is not spoken but felt, that is, we sense God in us, around us and in all Being.

If we want to learn to pray in the right way, much practice is necessary at first in order to become still. For this reason, when we first learn to pray, we should go to a quiet place where we are undisturbed, at best in the morning, before breakfast. With simple physical stretching exercises, which can be accompanied and supported by harmonious music, we attune our outer being, our body, as well as our inner being, our soul. Then we try to concentrate in this quiet, undisturbed place.

The following posture helps us to achieve the best physical relaxation and inner collectedness:

We sit on a straight-backed chair. Our torso rests upright on the coccyx. Both feet are on the floor. Our eyes are closed. We fold our hands in one another.

The left hand rests under the back of the right hand, and both palms are turned toward our body. In this way, we obtain a spiritual envelopment, in which the spiritual circulation is closed: Finger tips and palms do not radiate outward into our surroundings, but the energy flows back to the consciousness center located in the pelvic area. We remain still for some time in this posture and give over to the eternal Spirit our ever recurring thoughts.

To free ourselves from this flood of thoughts, which seems to overwhelm us again and again, we can also use a so-called consciousness aid which has a high vibration and helps us become more still, so that we can find our way deeper into our inner being. We say, for example, "Christ in me! Christ, may You become my life." Or "Harmony and peace draw into me. I am harmonious and peaceful."

In the beginning we consciously assume the described posture until it becomes a natural, harmonious prayer posture for us.

During prayer we try to penetrate from without to within, thus opening up the floodgates to true inner prayer. We now let our prayers of thankfulness and request flow inwardly to our spiritual consciousness. We continue to think the prayer into ourselves.

This prayer is still partly directed by our mind and flows, as mentioned, from without, from our person, from our brain cells, into our inner consciousness. Our prayer thoughts thereby touch our consciousness and our subconscious. They take along much to within, to the divine, into the realm of the inner being, where we express our concerns. The eternal power, which is active in the innermost part of our soul, then transforms many a thing which we place, consciously or unconsciously, upon the altar of divine love.

When first practicing the right prayer, we need a support and, as a help, an idea as to where we direct and send our prayers. And so, we can imagine the altar of God in our chest, near the fourth consciousness center. On this inner altar of love and mercy, we place our prayers of thankfulness and petition, the streams of our consciousness and subconscious.

Furthermore, we can imagine that the holy flame of God, the salvation-bringing flame of life, licks up from the region of consciousness of Order in the pelvic area, touching our thoughts of prayer and, transforming them into holy and positive energies, directing them to where they can find access and become effective.

The prayers which we still speak from our mind, and which we send inward, circle largely around our own interests. Only when we go more deeply into prayer, do we become aware that the entire fullness of infinity is in us and wants to become effective in us. When we then realize that we ourselves possess everything that we can open up through the right prayer and through a God-pleasing life, we will no longer ask, but will only give thanks.

Jesus said, "Ask and you will be given." In these words we recognize that He was speaking to people on the level of Order who may very well have borne the fullness of life within themselves, but had not yet unfolded it.

To pray within to the spirit of God, to the realm of the inner being, brings the unification with the spirit of God in the course of our life, for praying rightly is like living rightly. Whatever we do, we do in the awareness of God; that is the nearness of God; that is the stream which guides and vivifies us.

When, in this prayer, we have found our way within to God, to our inner consciousness—for the spirit of God dwells in us—then it will be possible for us to thank, praise and glorify God from within, in the course of our spiritual exercises.

Our prayers, too, will then become more selfless, and the spiritual consciousness will show us that what we ask for is in reality already in us and is already accomplished in us. God is in all things. He already knows our desires before we bring them to Him. Nevertheless, we may ask, in order to open up our inner being—the fullness that wants to become effective through us.

To pray within to God, to the holy consciousness, is a meditation of stillness, so to speak. When we pray, we should do it slowly and consciously. A forced prayer to achieve something or in the expectation of particular results is a fruitless prayer.

We should let the prayer thoughts vibrate into us slowly and harmoniously and should become accustomed to pausing briefly after each sentence. Through this, we become more still and find our way deeper into our spiritual consciousness, the God within.

When we pray quietly and let our prayer sensations and thoughts vibrate into us, placing them on the altar of God, as it were, then no specific breathing technique is needed. Through the brief pause after each thought or spoken sentence, through a totally relaxed and calm breathing and a conscious opening for the Spirit, we experience inner peace. We thereby experience a unique kind of deep meditation, because the divine source in us responds as soon as we address it from the deepest depths of our heart and filled with selfless love.

We should never forget that we are the temple of God and that the spirit of our Father dwells in us. When we cleanse this temple, in that our thoughts are noble and our speaking and acting are like our thoughts, then we will find our way to the Spirit, to the spirit of our Father—which not only dwells in the temple but also irradiates it.

The one who finds his way to loving by giving love will receive love in manifold ways. God, the eternal love, does not take. God is always the giving One. He, our Father, gives in abundance, for He is the fullness itself and also the fullness in us.

The Heart Prayer

The heart prayer is at an intermediate level. Heart prayers stream from the soul garments, which show the longings and desires of the person. The heart prayer is therefore the prayer from the soul garments, inspired by the soul particles, which bear human aspects that still show the person's burdens. The still existing longings and desires that rest in those deeper layers of the soul stream from there.

And so, the heart prayer is still a wish-prayer, which, however, is deeper and is not shaped by the mind alone. A person praying from the heart is still before the gate to eternal bliss. Heart prayers are like knocking at the gateway to the inner kingdom of peace and love. The small steps, the steadfast striving, the repeatedly renewed devotion to the eternal power bring spiritual success here, too. The gate will be opened one day to the one who continuously practices the right prayer and the right way of living; he will penetrate deeper to the core of being in his soul, to the eternal consciousness of God.

In love and adoration, we should offer consciousness aids and prayers, yes, our whole life, to Christ. He is our inner altar, our light and our life. He is the One who leads us to the Father. The inward journey to our inner life, to the origin of our being, is thus possible for everyone.

Through devotion and right prayer, we dissociate in our inner being from the world for some time. When we have secured the necessary and conscious distance from the world through contemplation and the right prayer, we can turn again toward the world in a new way.

However, we attain this solely with practice, discipline and concentration and through our love for God and our neighbor, by turning within consciously to the holy consciousness of God. In this way, we prepare our person and soul, because the right, deep and selfless prayer and a fulfilled, lawful life lead to unity with all Being.

And so, the person who journeys toward the kingdom of life, toward the inner homeland, is like a pilgrim who station by station draws closer to his inner God, to his inner homeland, thus attaining harmony and peace. The closer we come to the origin of the wellspring, the more we think and act from within, in accordance with the eternal laws. Through this, we become conscious beings of the Almighty, sons and daughters of God, who know about the inner life and who then are no longer of this world, even though they are still in the midst of the world.

Each person is given the possibility of leading a spiritual life in the midst of the world. The one who achieves this is completely transformed and secures a fulfilled existence through right prayer and a lawful life. A person who has untiringly practiced the heart prayer attains a harmonious body rhythm; his movements and gestures, speech and actions become more balanced and even.

However, the objective of our praying should not remain the heart prayer, the constant knocking at the gate of the kingdom of the inner being. Over the course of time, our prayer should become the soul prayer, because the gate to salvation should open so that we may approach the origin of our life.

When the heart prayer has been largely perfected, the gate to the inner God opens slowly, and from the soul stream the first impulses of life, which then intermingle with the prayer of the heart.

This means that someone who has learned to sink into himself, by having practiced the exercises to become still and silent, already experiences, to some extent, the streams from the soul, which intermingle with his heart-thinking and develop into a prayer.

When we have become people who think and pray from the heart, then the living power of our inner being springs from this, gushing forth like living water, free of emotion, unconstrained. Then praying brings joy and the longing to be in communion with God at every moment, the longing for the nearness to God.

Every not yet fully purified soul, every person burdened with his ego is an individual who thinks and lives according to his mentality and characteristics. This is why each person should pray in his own personal way, according to his present state of consciousness. And so, we should not imitate something which is not yet established in us; we should pray according to our own developed consciousness.

The right prayer is also a path of recognition; we recognize ourselves in our own prayer. As long as our prayer still contains desires and longings, we are still more or less strongly rooted in our ego. We can recognize and free ourselves through the right prayer, provided that we surrender to the all-power what we have recognized and that we observe the laws. Then, over the course of time, our prayer becomes selfless and a true melody of the inner being, which gushes forth from our secured, stable consciousness and attunes us anew, over and over again, inspiring us toward the higher.

We should not adhere to prayer formulas, because this has only a destructive effect on our own consciousness. We should pray according to our characteristics, to our feeling and thinking of the moment. And prayers which are usually said on certain occasions merely constrain us. The true seeker, the one who prays from his heart, who also recognizes himself in his prayer, will find his way to the inner source only when he prays freely, when he lets his consciousness pray. A free prayer springs from a loving heart and from a soul which opens itself for God, our Lord.

In order to let the prayer flow from our heart, we have to become still and turn off our thoughts completely. So that our thoughts move away from us, we listen to our breathing before praying and watch our body rhythm, which becomes more and more harmonious. Our breathing becomes calmer and our movements more harmonious, because the tormenting thoughts leave us. We reach a quiet body rhythm, because our breathing becomes deeper.

When we have been able to let go of our thoughts, when they have left us, we no longer watch our breathing or our body rhythm. We are now ready to pray from our heart, to let forces of love flow.

If it is not yet possible for us to pray the heart prayer, then we pray to within, until forces stir in our inner being which then pray through us. We pray into our inner being those things that burden and oppress us. We place our concerns on the altar of God.

Once we have reached inner stability, it will then pray within us. Selfless prayers will then rise without effort. It is a letting the inner powers come, which develop into prayer sensations and prayer thoughts. *It* prays through us.

This heart prayer, combined with the streams of the soul, characterizes the state in which our prayer becomes clearly one with our thinking, feeling and wanting. And so, it is no longer the prayer from the intellect but the prayer from the uppermost layers of our spiritual consciousness. This transition from strenuous prayer, with the thinking and formulating associated with it, to free and spontaneous prayer is a deep, unmistakable experience in the innermost part of our being.

We have to find our way to the depths of our being, where the awakened soul is in constant adoration of God. Then the prayer will speak in us, no matter where we are—in our quiet room or in the noisy world. *It* prays in and through us.

Then we have attained the nearness to God. The soul has awakened in God, and the person is aligned with God.

This means that soul and person are near the eternal consciousness, God.

The one who has practiced the heart prayer with utmost discipline and concentration and exercises to attain stillness senses the love of the all-ruling Spirit. Through the power of this love, he finds his way to this unceasing prayer, which rises at any time, any place, out of his inner being, giving thanks, honor and praise to God.

God is everywhere, for the spirit of God is in us and in everything that surrounds us. Nothing exists without the eternal power, God. For this reason, we can constantly speak with God, be it during housework, at our job, on the road, on a bus or train, or on a walk. In every activity, God, the all-power, is active in and around us.

When we act nobly and kindly, when our sensations and thoughts are pure, then this is likewise a prayer, for we fulfill the law of love. In this way, too, *it* prays through us.

Before we go to sleep or immediately after we awaken, *it* will pray in and through us, because our thought is like the thought of God. In this way, we find our way to true prayer, for each one of us should become the prayer.

The person who does these spiritual exercises of praying to within so that the gate to life may open, consciously and out of love for God, is grasped by the prayer, so that the whole person prays, no matter where he is. Only when we have become the prayer, do we actualize the laws in the right way, for the fulfillment of the holy laws is the same as the right prayer. There are enough people who pray regularly, who pray with their lips, but only a few who live in the nearness to God and have become the prayer.

On our pilgrimage to our inner God—which goes by way of becoming still, by way of the heart prayer, meditative absorption and a conscious, lawful life—we become capable of sensing and feeling ethereally. This means that we become more sensitive, more permeable to the eternal holy power. It is then possible for us to sense the substance of our true life in us, the holy power that is effective in all things.

We are beings of light and have to ascend again the ladder to heaven—which we once descended into the valley of tears and bitterness—in order to unite again with God, our Father. This ascension of the ladder of cosmic life is like a journey into the eternal Kingdom of God, which is within us.

We can climb the rungs to the cosmic consciousness only when we love God above all. The love of the Eternal then gives us the strength to live lawfully, to think and act in a disciplined way and to work with concentration, in order to thus become still through inner silence. Then, through the heart prayer and the soul prayer, we reach the ether prayer, which unites us completely with the Eternal.

By journeying into the kingdom of the inner being, we become selfless. The one who has become selfless no longer thinks of himself; he gives. Then our prayer, too, is similar. We no longer pray for our own interests. We know that we have everything, that the fullness offers itself to us every day. We pray for our neighbor, for the world, so that they may awaken and also find their way to the inner fullness, to God, who takes care of us, who is there for us. The inborn, cosmic, divine love then awakens more and more and gives us freedom and the deep peace which the world does not know, though many people seek it.

When we speak about the heart prayer, we do not mean the central anatomical organ, the physical heart of people, but the living life, the recognition that God exists. In sacrifice, we offer our thoughts and sensations to Him, so that it is not just our intellect, our human consciousness, or our subconscious that prays, but the streams of the awakened soul.

However, we do not want to stay with the heart prayer; this would be a standstill in our spiritual development. We want to reach the highest goal, the ether prayer, the constant nearness to God, yes, the fulfillment of what is lawful.

The heart prayer is like knocking at the inner gate which leads to the throne room of God, to His immediate heart. The heart prayer is only a preliminary step toward the soul prayer and the ether prayer. We want to strive for that highest goal, the unification with the consciousness of God.

A person who lives in the high, continuous adoration and in the praise of God, who thanks and praises Him for all things and fortune, lives in nearness to God. All things of life are revealed to him, for he has found his way to the inner truth.

When we have opened up the inner floodgates to the consciousness of God, when the gate to deeper bliss has opened, we will then advance toward the sensation of the soul, which conveys a high form of prayer to us.

When we have advanced into deeper areas of inner stillness, by praying the heart prayer into us and letting it rise back toward us, we then experience the prayer of the soul and heart, whereby soul and heart melt into one another. We could also describe this as follows: Filled with spiritual power, the consciousness and the subconscious are united with the soul. Soul and body worship the Godhead.

It should be our goal that our entire thinking, speaking and acting take place from the spiritual consciousness, that it thinks, speaks and acts through us. We will find our way to this high goal when we attune ourselves through ever deeper prayer, and by acting accordingly in our everyday life.

The further form of inner prayer is to take what we think and do and place it on our opened consciousness, on the spiritual potential that we have developed thus far and that has taken shape in us through a spiritual life. It will then be possible for us to live more and more in the kingdom of the inner being, and also to receive consciously from there for our material existence.

We then no longer live externally, tormented and chased by fear and opinions, marked by our way of thinking and acting and by our intellect, being dependent on them, but we live consciously from God, because God acts consciously through us. For He, the Almighty, directs our body, the matter, and our entire thinking and striving, thus guiding us. It, the life, guides us.

When we reach the nearness to God in our thinking, feeling, speaking and wanting, we will bear His holy name continuously and consciously in us. Then our prayers will increase in love, purity, selflessness, peace and obedience, and we will rise to further heights in order to pray in an even more fulfilled way.

The Soul Prayer

Complicated forms of prayer are tiring and distract us, because they come from human spheres, from our world of thoughts and senses, and are marked by our desires and longings. What has been acquired over years comes from outside. This also applies to prayer. What lies in the depths of our soul is spiritually inherent in us and comes from the pure regions of our soul. These innermost streams free the person and soul.

The path to the inner life demands a constant, critical observation of our feeling, thinking and acting. We have to avoid negative sensations and thoughts. They cloud our consciousness and bind us to external forms of prayer and to prayers which contain our own longings and desires. Then *it* no longer prays within us, but it is our intellect that prays. What the intellect produces does not bring about the nearness to God.

So that it may pray, think, speak and act through us, we have to watch our thoughts, to train our will, and to place our whole way of living under the salvation of the seal of divine love.

The spontaneous prayer of the soul flows only after a continuous, earnest and conscious struggle for the inner love and freedom.

Everything is grace; all things come from the giver of life. And so, the soul prayer, too, is a gift of God, which He grants to those who love Him more than this world. The soul prayer is the prayer of the selfless person. It cannot be achieved through certain techniques. It is given to the person who strives for the inner God in all earnestness and conscientiously examines and controls himself more and more, in order to become selfless.

The soul prayer is a prayer of the soul, heart and body. If we have attained a deep tranquillity and stillness, if we can remain silent in thoughts and words when our neighbor talks and boasts of his abilities and qualities, and if we can remain quiet in the midst of our daily life, in the bustle of this world, we have made great progress. We have taken a few steps toward self-mastery on the path to spirituality.

We will then be filled from within with strength and life and will continue to be oriented toward the highest goal. Through our increased strength, we will also be able to recognize the deeper-lying shadows of the human ego and to conquer them. We will then be fulfilled through our nearness to God and will pray from the soul, as it reveals itself there in the deeper regions of stillness.

When the soul has established a deep communion with God, our Father, in Jesus Christ, and is filled with His presence, then the person will rest more and more in God, his Lord. Then there is no need for consciousness aids, nor for observing our breathing and even less for certain forms of prayer. By way of deep stillness, the person increasingly receives the streams from the consciousness of the soul.

When heart and soul are filled with the omnipotence of God, they allow no more sinful thoughts or unlawful ideas.

When the person lives in the deep God-thought, then a transformation has taken place in his life. He has gained distance from the world in that—by becoming aware and overcoming—he loosened the ties which interwove him spiritually with the world, thus holding him captive. Strengthened and stabilized in his inner being, he can now approach the world again in a different way. Through such a life's transformation, with the right prayer and a lawful life, he has found the way which shows him, often after a long search, the possibility of a spiritual life in the midst of the world.

For the one who rests in God, there are no longer different kinds of people, but only children, sons and daughters of the eternal Father, who are on the way to the inner homeland. The one who lives in this high sensation of the all-unity is linked not only with people and beings, but with infinity. He beholds the life in all things and worships it. Thus, he is also close to the divine in nature. He feels himself to be the essence in every tree, in every bush, in every flower. He feels himself to be the essence in the stars, yes, in all Being, and he senses that the essence of all Being is in him.

This communication of forces, which is like a true communion, is the deep prayer, the prayer of the soul, which introduces the ether prayer.

A person who lives in this consciousness sees henceforth in everything only the ruling hand of the eternal laws. He radiates love and kindles love in his fellow man. He is above the vicissitudes of human life and is without fear. Nothing of low vibration penetrates him anymore. This high goal is reached step by step. His living and acting become the blessing from God, and his prayers are fruitful.

The soul prayer flows of itself. It streams from the inner being without effort. It is a selfless prayer, a prayer of tranquillity, of communion with the forces of love in the soul and in all Being. This prayer brings a hold and support, for it is not spoken by us, the intellect, but streams from our opened spirit-consciousness, from our present, regained spiritual potential of powers.

When the soul has absorbed the conscious prayer thoughts of Christ and is filled by His presence, the gate to the eternal life can also open further, so that ever more rays of divine love may penetrate it and fill the body of the person with light.

In the heart prayer and the soul prayer, we experience clearly and distinctly the statement: "I stand at the door and knock. If a person hears My voice and the door opens through prayer and love, I will enter, and I will be with him, and he will be with Me, and his meal will be My meal."

By praying within, by asking for strength, we come to the heart prayer, through which we find our way to the inner prayer, by letting *it* pray, so to speak. In this sequence—praying within and letting it pray—we come to the soul prayer. In this way, we come to the gateway, which the Lord Himself opens to us.

The soul prayer is no longer the heart prayer, in which the person and partial streams of the soul ask for their concerns and present their needs again and again. The soul prayer is much more. It embraces the entirety, because, through the person, the soul praises and glorifies God in Christ.

The pure soul prayer without side-inflows of the human will is an adoration and a veneration of the All-Highest, who knows about everything and is all things.

The soul prayer is deeply rooted. It senses, thinks, speaks and acts through me; it prays through me. The soul prayer is a praying from the developed consciousness, from the soul's spiritual potential of forces, which the person has actualized through a life in and with God. The first streams of the mentality of the inner being, of the spirit being, can be in the soul prayer.

In the last analysis, everything is filled and carried by the holy consciousness, God, the core of being of life; this is also true of the soul prayer. The spirit of God radiates into the soul, and the luminous being, the largely purified soul, shows its spiritual origin, its mentality, in prayer. The purer the soul is, the more selfless and sublime is the soul prayer.

The difference between the heart prayer and the soul prayer becomes very clear. The one who has found his way to the true soul prayer is selfless. He knows that all things are in him: He already has what he asks for; he already has what he wishes for.

Through these recognitions and by fulfilling the will of God, the person, the small, base ego, withdraws. The personal concerns withdraw and the awakened, luminous soul praises and thanks God. It speaks to Him in pure and noble sensations, thoughts and words.

If what is noble, pure and beautiful goes out from us, we increasingly find our way to the deep, genuine, selfless soul prayer. The awakened soul continuously thanks God, God, the Giver, who is the gift at the same time, since He unites all good things in Himself. If we are ill, He is our healer. If we are hungry, He feeds us. If we are cold, He warms us. If we are accused, He defends us. If we are insulted, He comforts us. If we are persecuted, He is our rescue. If we fall, He picks us up. If we doubt, He strengthens us. If we become inconsistent and weak, He gives us courage.

From all this we recognize that we are limbs on the spiritual body of Christ and, at the same time, cells on His spiritual body. When His name is close to us, when we are constantly linked with Him in thought, that is, when our sensations and thoughts are pure, we will be imbued by His holy power. A person who recognizes His ruling hand in everything communicates with the holy forces, which are active in the minerals, in the plants, in the animals and especially in human beings.

God lives through the one who lives in Him, and He lets become manifest everything that the soul hides from the one who aspires only to outer things, and lives externally.

When the person has found his way to this power of prayer, he is filled with the natures and attributes of God and becomes the prayer little by little. The one who has become the prayer is self-less and is no longer marked by his ego. The one who rests in God, his Lord, has surrendered his ego to the I Am, to the great Spirit, who knows all things.

In God, human things are unimportant and trivial. What is important is the law, which is the fullness and produces the fullness in us. A person who lives in the fullness of God is fearless, for he lives in the truth. God is the truth.

The one who strives toward God will, in the course of his becoming, let go of everything unessential that keeps him away from the divine stream of salvation, distracting him and wanting to drag him down into the world of illusions.

The one who wants to prepare his whole soul for the deep prayer, the soul prayer, should send awakening impulses over and over again into his innermost being, into the soul, such as:

Father,
You are my innermost consciousness!
Holy and mighty is Your eternal love.
Through the consciousness of Your Son, Jesus Christ, I experience Your holy natures and attributes in myself. Your "Let there be" streams through my soul, so that I may become what I am from the very beginning.
Let me become the prayer; let me be wholly Your own.
My soul, lift your voice in praise of the One who created you. May my soul

praise, glorify and thank the Lord, the Almighty, who is all things and in everything.

Hallowed is His name. I sanctify His name, so that I may be divine again through His name, God.

Resting in our innermost being, turned away from external phenomena, we listen to the impulses of the soul. Patient and ready, without wanting anything and totally prepared for God, we await the prayer of our soul.

Our linking in thought with the eternal Spirit in us brings us closer to the Omnipresence. If we call His name fervently, God will answer us. He places His word into the soul, and the person aligned with God may perceive the voice of God.

If the soul has taken in the thought about the Christ of God and is filled with His presence, then every thought will be the thought of Christ, for every thought is a thought of salvation, noble and pure. There is then no need to constantly repeat the name of Christ, for we live in Him and He lives through us.

It is advisable to repeat the name of God and Christ only when we are drawn to without by the events of this side of life. When we come into need, despair or fear, we should speak out the name "God-Father" or "Christ," filled with calm and hope, trusting in the Omnipotence that we will receive what we ask for. This invocation is successful only when we ask selflessly, not wanting to force anything with our request, but placing it before the Omnipotence, so that it can be done according to His will.

When we are led into temptation by the world, by external forms, images and impressions, we should call on the name of God and Christ persistently but calmly and should turn our thoughts away from the external influences. We let the melody "Father" or "Christ" resound in our heart and in our soul until all thoughts of doubt, fear, anxiety and all negative feelings stream out of our inner being and we again sense the inflow of the all-power and, renewed and strengthened, we may receive His light and His voice.

It is a blessing to be united with the Eternal! When we are close to God in our thoughts, we feel the rescuing hand of the Almighty at every moment. When we do not just keep His name on our lips, but let it flow through our whole being, then the might and power of the divinity becomes visible through us, because our life is marked by spiritual success.

We will fulfill in the world what is for the benefit of our neighbor, for his soul. This inner divine power of love will then also rule our whole physical body and will strengthen and invigorate us. It keeps away from us what characterizes the world, illness, need and sorrow. The fulfillment of the holy laws purifies our soul, our heart and our body, and sanctifies our being.

Equipped with these forces, we will pray more and more consciously, and will eventually find our way to the ether prayer, in which we are absolutely filled with the omnipresent power of God. Through this development of prayer and by fulfilling the spiritual life, we find our way more and more to the eternal consciousness, to the core of being of God in our soul.

When we let go of our humanness, our base ego, and lead a conscious inner life, we find our way to the unification with God and will be consciously in God, and God will be consciously in us, and we will become the law, the being, the divine being, which was created by God.

The Ether Prayer

The ether prayer is the recognition and at the same time the absolute fulfillment of the holy laws of God.

With our daily effort to please God, we penetrate ever deeper into the kingdom of our inner being. By going steadily within toward our inner God, toward the kingdom of the inner being, about which Jesus said, "My kingdom is not of this world," we come to ever greater regions of sublime stillness and deep peace.

When there is no more struggle with ourselves, our soul has become still, and we rest in God, our Lord. We can then say consciously and with absolute certainty, "It is not I who live, but it is Christ who lives and works through me."

In this inspiring state of true, deep stillness and divine joy, we climb the last slope toward the absoluteness, toward the perfect truth. In this state of permanent inwardness, we can stand in the greatest turmoil, in the noisy world, and yet remain quiet, turned into our inner being, for our soul has become still. It rests in God, its Lord, who created it. Then it is no longer we who live, but *it* lives through us.

The person who experiences this state of unity with God is united from within with the absolute consciousness, God. He is guided by God, the all-power, without the interference of his soul garments and of his consciousness and subconscious.

Then it is not we who think and act, but *it* feels, thinks, speaks and acts through us. And so, we become the true prayer; we become the law itself, which lasts forever, for the eternally holy law of love created us. We came from it and must find our way back to it, and become absolute law.

We attain the tranquillity and inner stability, yes, the stillness of our soul, only by purposely going within to our eternal consciousness, which waits for us, as it were, which calls us, and which we should become again. By going within to our holy consciousness, to God, our eternal Father, by way of the heart prayer and the soul prayer and the fulfillment of the inner life, we experience the presence of the Father and of the Son in us and in every person.

The one who lives in Christ finds himself in the true church, for man is the temple of the Holy Spirit. Therefore, the one who enters the temple, by purifying it and sanctifying it, is, himself, the church of Christ.

Through this life from the inner being, we experience more and more the great unity in God. We experience that all life comes from His holy consciousness, that He is the life in all things. The one who experiences this depth, the stillness of his soul, knows that he is linked in love with those who already live in the beyond and are going toward further liberation and development. In this way, we grow more and more into the unity of God and ultimately become the unity.

During this steady blossoming in the holy law of God, we come to know and experience the presence of all life more each day, and from this we recognize that everything is in us and we are in everything. The one who experiences this and attains the fulfillment from the stream of life has found his way home.

Through this knowledge, the fulfillment and the awakening in the eternal law of unity, of divine love, we come to know and experience ever deeper peace and inspiring harmony, for we draw closer to the origin of the wellspring, to the Absolute.

In the divine peace and divine harmony, which are also the stillness of our inner being, the garments of humanness fall from us more and more. Fear, vanity and blind egocentricity are far from us, for we have become the true and deep prayer.

This becoming brings us selflessness, because we are consciously born in God, just as Christ, the Redeemer-Spirit, is born in us.

We then approach our fellow man with our sensations more than with our thoughts, whether in the street, in the office, in the store, in the factory or in the automobile.

We recognize Christ in all people, even in those whom we find unpleasant and do not like. When we see Christ even in our apparent enemies, when we see our brother and sister in them, then we show greatness and may say, "We are becoming one with the holy primordial principle; we are drawing closer to the origin of the wellspring."

The inner stillness tells us: Honor your heavenly Father in Christ and serve Him in each one of your fellow men; for the spirit of your Father in Christ, the redeeming flame that brings salvation, implanted through the sacrifice on Golgotha, dwells in all men and women, even in the ill-natured ones and in criminals.

Let us become aware that we are all brothers and sisters and that we will meet one day again in the eternal home-land, as pure children of the eternal Father! If we strive for this already now on earth, then in the spheres beyond we will have nothing more to forgive and nothing to be forgiven for. We will be free in God and happy in the eternal homeland, which is our eternal dwell-ing place.

Therefore, we should endeavor to address Christ in our neighbor, no mat-ter what his attitude toward us is, by silently acknowledging and worship-ping Christ in our neighbor. Then our humanness will recede more and more, and we will see our brother and our sister in Christ through our spiritual eyes.

If we go through the world with this spiritual attitude and say only good and noble things about our fellow man, if we see in everything the holy ruling hand of God, the ruling of His heavenly laws, and if we strive to fulfill them in ourselves, with our neighbor and also with the nature kingdoms, we will then walk in the law of the Almighty, thus fulfilling the ether prayer: "I am in God, and God is consciously in me, acting through me."

The more we are ready to recognize the ruling hand of God in all things, to thank Him, praise and glorify Him and bear His name in our heart and on our lips, the more radiant our soul becomes, the brighter our nature. We then fulfill what the Almighty wishes of us, His children, that we subdue the earth in love. This is deep prayer; this is the ether prayer.

The one who lives in the ether prayer lives henceforth from within. His inner homeland is already wide open to him. From now on, his sensing, thinking, speaking, feeling and acting take place via his expanded and stabilized mental and spiritual consciousness.

What he thinks and says is no longer his intellect, his mind, but his innermost consciousness, the law of the soul. The active consciousness of our soul then acts on our physical consciousness and conveys the inner life to us. The conscious child of God, living in the "I am the son or the daughter of the Most High," then faithfully fulfills the impulses of his soul.

The person who so lives in the divine consciousness will think and speak only good and essential things. His speech is no longer directed by his mind. Although he speaks with the words of this world, it is nevertheless a different language, a thoroughly spiritualized and ennobled language, which streams, so to speak, from his inner being. It is the language of the divine consciousness.

The one who wants to cast off the shackles forged by error shall walk this path of prayer and of the fulfillment of the holy laws. Only so does the God-seeker find his way to the absolute truth; and his soul, which has become the spirit body, will see God, its Father, face to face after this sojourn in the temporal. The one who has the fervent faith in the inner might and power of the eternally Holy One and consciously bears Him day and night in his heart needs no further spiritual exercises.

It is possible for the one who lives in the ether prayer to expound on the various spiritual paths and to lead seekers onto the right path.

The true Christian, who lives from his opened inner consciousness, recognizes that in the end all paths lead to Christ and through Christ to the Father. If Christ has risen in us, we will be kind to all people.

The absolute ether prayer, the deep true prayer, is to pray without knowing it any longer, because one continuously fulfills the holy laws. We then live constantly in the spirit of truth; we feel, think and speak from the inner truth. Our actions rise from the truth.

Then there will be no more hollow and flat expressions, no empty forms, no lies, no sentimentality. Our sensations and impulses will then be true, as true as every tear which is shed when the sweetness and glory of God completely permeates us. The tears then become pearls which show us the way to the absolute Omnipotence. They bring us strength and higher spirituality.

But without an inner struggle, we will not find the way to our inner life, to the deep stillness of God. We are called upon to struggle with our weaknesses and faults. However, with the inner power, with the power of Christ, we will conquer ourselves, thus becoming blessed people who want to bless all people, not with many words, not through fanaticism, but through a conscious life and by explaining the true inner religion.

When we constantly think of God in our soul, in our heart and on our lips, we have become the prayer and stand before the absolute unification with the eternal Being, with God, our Father. Then, the soul, our purified body, will call through us, "Father, I place my spirit in Your hands. It is accomplished through Christ."

The Healing Prayer

Pray yourself healthy! The best help for your health, which is life force, is positive, noble sensations and thoughts. The nobler and purer your inner attitude, the more forces of healing and life you awaken.

Christ, the spark of life in you, is the power of healing and life in your soul and in your body. When you unlock the inner gate to the Kingdom of God with the redeeming power of Christ, by affirming salvation, yes, the powers that heal, and by fulfilling the holy laws, then you will also receive. Pray yourself healthy!

Let every sensation, every thought and every word become a prayer! Then the gate to life will open, and you will be filled with strength, wisdom, love and health.

It is written, "Ask and it will be given unto you." However, the request should not be just the expression of an external affirmation, a calling or a lip prayer. The request should come from the fulfillment of the holy laws, from the affirmation of the inner power through a noble way of feeling, thinking and wanting.

The eternal life force streams incessantly from the origin of the wellspring. If we are willing to accept it, by fulfilling the laws, we receive this healing and life-giving power via the core of being of our soul. We can increase the inflow of this healing and life-giving power many times over, if we affirm these forces of life and fulfill them in our everyday life, since they are the laws of life. When we knock at the gate to the eternal life, by lifting our heart toward God, the gate will open and we will receive.

The inner prayer to the Inner Physician and Healer requires a strong faith and a deep trust in the One who is capable of everything, who is everything. To become healthy means to become healthy through the power of the Inner Physician and Healer.

The spirit of God knows no illness; and according to our origin, we are pure beings who bear within all the powers of salvation. As beings of light, we are not ill. We are ill because of our wrong thinking, feeling and wanting, because of our violations of the law. However, it has been given to us by Christ to be able to address the inner powers, to activate them and also to guide them to our ill or ailing organs, for according to our origin, we are children of God.

Since we are children of the eternal life, sons and daughters of God, it is given to us to guide the forces of healing and of life to every organ, to every muscle, to our whole organism through the right prayer and by addressing the organs. Each one of us can communicate with his cells and organs, for the spiritual power is in every cell. The more intensively we affirm this inner power through strong faith and total trust, through positive thoughts, noble sensations and the fulfillment of the holy laws, the more we will receive.

With conscious inner prayer, with positive sensations and thoughts, the reveille is sounded to our cells and organs, to our entire organism. When we incessantly affirm the inner powers, the powers of healing and of life, with our opened consciousness—that is, in full affirmation—then a change occurs in us. The Inner Physician and Healer, the spirit of Christ, then becomes increasingly active.

The eternal power, Christ, just waits until we are willing to open the inner gate with Him through the power of right prayer and right will, in order to thus surrender to the inflow of the eternal divine potential.

We are cells on the body of Christ. Our body cells are ill merely because we have weakened them through wrong thinking, feeling and wanting, thus letting in certain illnesses. When we send positive, healthy, light-filled thoughts to our cells, organs, our tissues and muscles, our hormones and glands, we will then receive from the eternal source of life according to our devotion.

And so, the best help for your health is positive, selfless thoughts; they are the building material for a healthy body. When we affirm our physical health every day, no illness can enter us, since there is no correspondence in us, unless the illness is conditioned by karma.

When we fall ill, recovery is always granted to us, if it is good for our soul. If we open up the inner gate to life with Christ, through the affirming life that God wants, we will receive, for the Inner Physician and Healer dwells in us. He waits for our call, for our devotion, for the actualization and fulfillment of the laws, because then the gate opens, and the life flows as a stream throughout our body, bringing us relief and healing.

The love of God for His child is unchangeable. It is not He, the almighty love, who sends to us suffering and affliction. These are based solely on the all-ruling and all-valid law of cause and effect, on the law of justice. In this or one of our previous lives, we created causes, having offended the law. We have to accept and bear whatever we cause, so that the way back to the light-filled eternal origin, to the eternal homeland, can be walked again.

A soul-debt which, according to iron-clad laws, flows out during our life, bringing us illness, need, worries or blows of fate, can nevertheless be healed or relieved, depending on the severity of the karma. To what extent it can be paid off depends solely on us, on how we surrender ourselves to the Inner Physician and Healer, to the spirit of Christ, whether with full trust and faith in Him, the Almighty, or with doubt that He can really help and heal us. Every doubt is a setback in our life. It closes us and cements over the gate which leads to the Inner Physician and Healer. Affirming, conscious, single-minded God-thoughts lead us to success.

The condition of our body is the expression of our soul, of our present or former sensing, thinking, feeling and wanting. What we think today is what we are in our inner being; it is our nature; it is the thoughts we have thought into this or a former life. In this way, we created the correspondence in us, the burden of our soul.

No illness comes of itself; it is always caused by us. The so-called chronic illnesses are also visible manifestations of our previous or present negative thoughts. If we want to bring about a change, we should think of the Inner Physician and Healer and entrust ourselves to Him, by persistently and consciously having positive thoughts, thus mobilizing the inner forces.

Healing prayers are mostly prayers of request. They should stream from the depths of our consciousness; then they are powerful and can bring healing. However, when we pray and request, we should not beg.

A wailing request for this or that, for health and strength does not take place in the consciousness of true, sincere humility; it is not addressed to the great Giver, who would like to grant

His child all the good that it needs. However, the omnipotent, omniscient spirit of God knows best what is helpful and beneficial for us at present. And so, we do not ask a God who first has to be well-disposed and favorably inclined toward us to grant our request, but should ask our heavenly Father, whose spirit we know dwells in us. We should fully trust Him, no matter whether He considers our soul alone, or both our soul and body. When we affirm His eternal power thankfully and gladly, it will also fulfill us.

The spirit of love is the power of our life. It is the healing power for soul and body. This power alone lets us become happy, healed and perfect.

The healing prayer should not be limited to a prayer of request, but should become a continuous affirmation of the divine energies in us.

We should not grant access to any thought of despair, weakness, sorrow or lack of faith. They merely weaken our soul and our body. Our consciousness and subconscious, the surface of the inner sea, should become calm, so that the inner sun is able to heal us.

When we become accustomed to replacing thoughts of sadness, fear, desperation, hopelessness, despondency and self-pity with positive, affirmative thoughts, then we will also receive a positive harvest. For the sunny brightness of our life lets the inner sun shine more intensely into our body, to our cells, organs and muscles.

As long as we see ourselves as human beings and think as human beings, we have only the powers of human beings. But when we acknowledge ourselves as children of the Almighty, as divine beings, when we think in a positive and noble way and orient our thinking and striving toward God, we gain the powers of our infinitely eternal Being. We may rely on God, our Father, for we are sons and daughters of God.

The healing prayer is the free affirmation of health, which is our God-given right since the divine being, which we are in our innermost being, is healthy. Even when pain torments us, when our soul is clouded, we should nevertheless think into ourselves forces of health, affirming, positive, constructive thoughts. This is the best medicine; it is the forces not yet scientifically explored, which become effective in our inner being.

A healing prayer may read as follows:

In me is the spirit of Christ, the absolute eternal power.
Within me stream the wellsprings of life.
I am healthy.
I am a child of this eternal power. God's life is in me, and my life is in God.
God's fullness is effective in me. God is the fullness and the power. God is my health. His holy and healing power floods through my soul and my body and makes everything new.
My cells, organs, hormones and glands, the muscles and tissues are permeated

by the spiritual power and pervaded by the holy life forces.

I affirm this eternal power in me and open myself each day more for the life in me through affirming, constructive sensations and thoughts.

Weakness and illness do not touch me, for my eternal being is healthy. I am healthy; I am cheerful and strong.

I feel the increasing inflow of the divine fullness. The eternally bubbling wellspring fulfills itself in me. I receive from it increased strength, health and fullness.

All thoughts of worry and fear withdraw from me. They become ever weaker and dissolve in the all-harmony of my Father.

From my inner being rises the divine stillness. I am permeated by the inner stillness and all-harmony.

Vivified by this inner calm, I turn increasingly toward the inner healing power. The healing and life-forces flow through me more each day. The Redeemer-Spirit, Christ, is effective in me, my Inner Physician and Healer.

My hands and arms relax; the muscles of my legs loosen. My whole body, my throat, neck and head, all the muscles relax. My body becomes lighter and lighter. The fullness of divine salvation streams into me. Healing forces of love activate me. My breathing is calm; I am totally relaxed. Inner tranquillity and harmony flood through my being. Christ, You, my Inner Physician and Healer, may Your will be done in me.

After this healing prayer, we remain in the stillness. No sensation and no thought streams through us. We are and remain open to the healing forces of Christ.

So that no thoughts find access to us, we may watch our breathing while absolutely relaxed, how it comes and goes again. With every inhalation, the divine power streams into our inner being; with every exhalation, the heaviness and burden, our still existing human weaknesses and afflictions, dissipate.

It is done in us according to His will. In us the Inner Physician and Healer accomplishes the work of His love and mercy.

After the healing prayer and being in the stillness, we should no longer let ourselves be dominated by our old habits. We should strive to affirm all the positive forces that we have set free in our inner being with further prayers that bring healing and through a positive life. When we avoid every negative thought, any thought of illness and affliction, we experience increased spiritual power. We experience the inner healing power, which gives us relief and healing.

Many of our fellow men think they have to visit a place of healing in order to be healed from their ailments. Our unknowing brothers and sisters travel many miles to such places. They take this trouble in order to perhaps attain relief or healing there. But the person who knows that the place of inner strength is in himself—from which he can receive what is good and beneficial for him—needs only to go on a pilgrimage to within, to the inner place of holy stillness and eternal peace, in his inner being, where the wellspring of healing and of life flows.

Whether we are in a place of healing or anywhere else, the power is always the same. It is not outside our being, but in us. Wherever we are, wherever we go, the source of healing for all life, the strength to attain health, is in us. Within us is the spring of health, the Spirit.

When cases of spontaneous healing take place in such places of healing, it is only because the person makes a pilgrimage there with the certainty of a strong faith, in order to attain healing there. If the one seeking healing would make a pilgrimage to the inner place of grace, to the inner source of healing, with the same trust and vivified by this deep faith, he could also receive relief and healing from his inner being.

The power of life flows eternally in the same way, at any place and any time. God, the source of life, is not tied to any place. The divine stream is omnipresent. God, the eternal Spirit, gives Himself to His children.

We have to recognize and acknowledge that the power for becoming healed is in us. It is granted to us only if we open ourselves for it. What hinders us from obtaining relief and healing is above all our lack of faith. Jesus could hardly bring about a healing in Nazareth, His hometown, because the Nazarenes did not believe in Jesus, who had grown up there.

All things are possible to the one who believes and fulfills the divine laws. The harvest always corresponds to the sowing.

If the sowing of positive and trusting thoughts is scanty, the result of relief and healing is scanty as well. Another hindrance is doubt. The one who doubts does not look into his inner being, but looks to the left and right. He keeps a lookout into this world, looking to become healed. Many people waver between believing and disbelieving, because they have not been taught since childhood that they are the temple of the Holy Spirit and that the source of all Being, the wellspring of healing, flows in them. Through this, the person sets up barriers against the divine inflow. He searches externally for relief and healing and mostly cannot find what his soul needs.

How quickly we become discouraged when our prayers are not immediately heard as we would like or as we had experienced before! Let us remember how long we have sinned against the holy laws, thus creating a gap between the divine power and our own thinking and feeling. The Holy Spirit does not act immediately, for it is necessary that we ourselves conquer this gap so that the healing streams can flow.

Besides, not every day is like another, and we ourselves are not the same every day. In us, in our inner being, there are many kinds of changes which are partially concealed to us, and which can also erect a barrier against the inflow of the healing power in us.

The right prayer, a deep prayer, is indeed important in order to be heard. However, we should not want to score goals, for prayer is not a sport, but devotion.

Let us help to make order again in our inner being by continually bearing God-thoughts in our heart and on our lips, by doing everything with God, and praising His holy name, His holy law, which prevails in all things! Many a knot, which may have hardened during our long years on earth or even over many incarnations, can only be carefully loosened with divine patience, love and mercy.

For this reason we should not be discouraged, but should seek the nearness of God every moment by intensifying the inner feeling that God is close to us, in our heart and in all Being.

Someone who builds on earthly help more than on the divine becomes insensitive to the holy and healing stream. We also limit our becoming healthy through our restless consciousness and subconscious.

We often lack the love for God and thus the love for our neighbor, which we need in order to attain relief and healing. How often is it impossible for us to forgive—even in our thoughts. We cannot get rid of our thoughts, feelings, mistrust, bitterness, envy, hatred and lust for power because, based on disappointments, we have created all these weaknesses, which we now want to keep.

We think that our neighbor should come to us, speak with us, and apologize. But the one who shows greatness goes to his neighbor and speaks with him, so that many things can be solved. In this way, we give the healing powers the possibility to flow in.

By not wanting to forgive, by maintaining our individuality and our hurt feelings, we shut ourselves off from the healing forces. If we want to receive the healing power from the spirit of life, we have to let go of these barriers of mistrust, bitterness, envy, hatred and jealousy, even those of hurt feelings. We should give all this over to the Eternal to be transformed, so that we may become receptive to the eternal power.

We should recognize and discard these shackles with which we have fettered ourselves and which now hold us captive, by giving them over to the

Eternal for transformation. No external walls can confine us as painfully as those of our limited consciousness, created by our own fault.

Wherever we erect barriers of inner constraint, the spiritual stream cannot flow intensively. These barriers must fall, so that we can receive the eternal power.

When we learn to become tolerant, to discard our mistrust, our hatred and our lust for power, we can forgive and master our thoughts and sensations. We then receive the divine power. The healing power of the Inner Physician and Healer flows into us and brings about what people are not capable of.

The inner power can heal any illness. For God, no illness is incurable. The person who surrenders himself to the eternal law, to the Inner Physician and Healer, is properly guided and can receive according to his alignment, that is, according to his actualization of the holy laws.

For God nothing is impossible. Relief and healing are possible in every case, if we just affirm the unlimited healing power of God and trustingly let it become effective in us. In all our prayer requests, in all our desires and yearnings which we bring within to the holy consciousness of God, we should not forget to speak in full awareness, "But Your will be done, O Lord!"

God is there whenever we need help, for He is omnipresent. Let us become aware of the depth of these words, God is there!

God is there wherever we are and go. He is merely waiting for us to turn our inner being into a receiving station for His holy life, for God sends powers upon powers untiringly, energies of healing and of life.

When we have become a receiving station for these life forces, the divine healing power, His power of grace, is then constantly active in us. The more developed this inner receiving station, the more we receive the divine life. The Spirit of our soul is ready and willing at every moment to give to us, yes, to give Itself. There are countless examples of God having manifested His love and wisdom. Many people know about this and have experienced and received His help, His healing power.

We, too, should become the conscious revelation of God by devoting ourselves to the all-power, God, asking for His holy inflow and fulfilling the eternal laws. Then we will come to know and experience and become one with the eternal wellspring.

This I wish with all my heart for all my fellow men!

Books from the Universal Life Series

This Is My Word
A and Ω
The Gospel of Jesus
The Christ-Revelation
which the world does not know
1078 pages / Order No. S 007en

The Sermon on the Mount
Life in accordance with the law of God
(an excerpt from "This Is My Word")
117 pages / Order No. S 008en

The INNER PATH, Collective Volume
The Original Christian School of Life
The Inner Path to Becoming One
with the Spirit of God In Us
7 books in one / 1344 pages / Order No. S150en

The Great Cosmic Teachings of
JESUS of Nazareth
to His Apostles and Disciples
Who Could Understand Them.
With explanations by Gabriele in the Great
Teaching Church of the Spirit of God
(Vol. 1) 255 pages / Order No. S 317en

For a free catalog of all our books,
cassettes and videos,
please contact:

Universal Life
The Inner Religion
PO Box 3549
Woodbridge, CT 06525, U S A
Tel. 203-458-7771 • Fax 203-458-0713
1-800-846-2691

Verlag DAS WORT GmbH
im Universellen Leben
Max-Braun-Strasse 2
97828 Marktheidenfeld/Altfeld, Germany
Tel. 9391-504-132 • Fax 9391-504-133

E-mail: info@universelles-leben.org
Website: http://www.das-wort.com